ORGANISING PRODUCTIVE WORKSHOPS

Work together to achieve your goals

ORGANISING PRODUCTIVE WORKSHOPS

Work together to achieve your goals

Written by Maïlys Charlier
Translated by Jessica Foster

ORGANISING PRODUCTIVE WORKSHOPS

- **Issue:** how can I prepare a workshop and achieve my objectives in a few steps?
- **Uses:** a good group dynamic leads to better learning and stimulates individual creativity.
- **Professional context:** training, introducing new staff members, team building, professional reorientation, teamwork.
- **FAQs:**
  - What are the golden rules for an effective workshop?
  - How do I choose the participants?
  - How can I organise a workshop that is several days long?
  - How do I keep the participants motivated throughout the event?
  - How can I manage unforeseen circumstances during the workshop?
  - How important is the debriefing?
  - What qualities must a good organiser have?
  - What technical aspects must be taken into account?

What is a workshop? You have undoubtedly heard this word before, but its meaning may still seem a little vague to you. It is not, as you might think, anything to do with shopping. It is in fact an event at which several specialists and amateurs come together to work on a precise, predefined topic. At a time in which project management and team leading are developing considerably in businesses, workshops can be an indispensable and extremely useful tool.

Would you like to train your team in new technologies? Refresh your social media skills? Standardise your business's marketing strategy? Workshops can help you to reach new objectives. Indeed, this interactive gathering promotes the exchange of ideas between experts and beginners. All you have to do is decide on a subject, invite appropriate people and get everyone talking. And what better way to learn about a speciality than to discuss it with professionals?

Starting now, this short guide will teach you how to plan and organise an effective workshop thanks to the keys to success!

ORGANISING A WORKSHOP: THE BASICS

What is the point of a workshop?

There are many benefits of a workshop:

- informing people and making knowledge accessible
- learning new skills
- developing creativity
- innovating
- resolving specific problems.

Within a company, a workshop can be organised in order to more easily find a solution to a recurring problem or to explore a new way of working. For example, in order to redefine a company's web strategy, a workshop can bring together all the people in the company who are involved in this area (IT technicians, analysts, community managers, communications supervisors, etc.). It therefore has a double function: reinforcing a feeling of belonging to the team and motivating employees.

Creating a 'work bubble'

Group dynamic is one of the essential elements of a good workshop, as the team's cohesion and the project's success depend on it. As the management specialists Anca Metiu and Nancy P. Rothbard point out in a study published in 2012 entitled *Task Bubbles, Artefacts, Shared Emotion, and*

Mutual Focus of Attention: A Comparative Study of the Microprocesses of Group Engagement, a workshop will be more effective and productive if a work bubble is created. The two authors illustrate that problem resolution tends to happen after interactions within small, temporary groups in which there is a strong group engagement.

This work bubble allows the group to stay solid and not be influenced by external factors. The participants, generally assembled into small groups, learn more quickly due to this group dynamic; information is more easily assimilated, which allows increased motivation and creativity of each individual. During your workshop, try to increase the number of interactions and encourage collaboration among participants in order to create this bubble.

The key players

In order for your workshop to work, you also need to enlist the help of experts who will share their experience and know-how. An organiser must be present to coordinate the activities, supervise the participants and assist the experts. For shorter workshops (a few hours long), usually only one organiser is needed. They will manage the schedule and announce when the session is over. If a workshop is longer than one day, it is essential to have additional help, preferably in the form of a communications specialist. This second person will be in charge of the participants and the logistics of the workshop so that the organiser is free to prepare the sessions.

Is a short or long workshop preferable?

Depending on your needs and objectives, the length of the workshop may vary from a few hours to several days.

- The shorter the workshop, the more necessary it is for the organiser(s) to be well-prepared and attentive in order to create this work bubble, which is essential to the workshop's success.
- The longer the workshop, the more depth the subject will be explored in. This also gives the participants time to get to know each other better, talk and ask the experts their questions. Obviously, if the workshop will last several days, breaks will be necessary so that the work sessions are not too intense.

THINGS TO AVOID

To avoid a bad atmosphere settling over a group, the organiser needs to ensure that they are maintaining a positive dynamic overall. Indeed, if some participants are not motivated or are afraid to put forward their ideas, the negative effect can spread to all the other individuals.

The 7Ps theory

The 7Ps theory, put forward by James Macanufo, one of the authors of the famous work Gamestorming, allows us to identify the essential elements of a workshop.

- **Purpose:** what is the workshop's purpose? Why has it been organised?
- **People:** who will be there? What are their targets? What are everyone's roles?
- **Product:** in what way will it be beneficial?
- **Process:** what activities are planned? What is the workshop's schedule?
- **Preparation:** should the participants do some preparation work? Do you need to provide documents for them to do this?
- **Practical concerns:** what do you have to think about in terms of logistics? Do you have to book a room? Do you need catering?
- **Pitfalls:** what risks are there? How should you manage or avoid them?

everything for the participants and experts.

- Do not succumb to stress: this will help you to better manage potential conflicts or unforeseen circumstances. *"When organising a workshop, there are endless questions and problems. You have to be able to resist stress to deal with the situation and quickly propose solutions." (Abigail, event organiser)*
- Show empathy, as this will have an effect on the participants' moods.
- Be dynamic, as this will engender a positive atmosphere and constant motivation in the working groups.
- Be versatile. You will have to carry out many of the tasks yourself (plugging in the video projector, printing the documents, setting up the room, ordering taxis, making coffee, etc.). Being adaptable will be an asset!

THE VARIOUS STEPS TO FOLLOW

Preparation

- **Write a checklist.** On it, write every phase of preparation and the elements that they are composed of. It will be a guide for when the organisation of the workshop is progressing.
- **Give the workshop a clear and attractive title,** once the subject has been set, so that it is easily understood by everyone. For example: 'Getting your start-up off the ground', 'Redefining your company's online strategy',

'Optimising your marketing plan', 'Using social media to promote your company'. If your title is vague, people will be less likely to sign up.

- **Define your objectives.** Determine which abilities and skills you would like the participants to develop. For example: mastering social media, being able to set out a marketing strategy, etc. Once you have fixed your objectives, you will know how to orientate your workshop and you will avoid affecting the work with off-topic subjects.
- **Choose and invite experts,** professors or professionals who will be the most apt at meeting the participants' demands and expectations. For example, invite a Mark Zuckerberg-type character to a workshop about launching a start-up, ask social networking specialists to reveal their secrets during a workshop on social networks, suggest several marketing experts for a workshop on optimising a business's marketing strategy, etc. It is important to instruct and inform the experts, so that they are aware of the topics to discuss. Moreover, maintaining good communication with them is essential, both on a material level (projector, technological devices, documents to print, etc.) and a logistic level (transport, hotels, food, schedule, etc.).
- **Choose the participants.** You need to be sure that all the participants are motivated to come to the workshop. Ask for a letter of motivation and, potentially later on, carry out interviews with the candidates in order to select the most highly-motivated. It is important to open sign-ups enough in advance – without forgetting to notify the candidates of how and when to pay – if you want to have enough participants on the day. Include additional time

to collect everyone's payments.

- **Choose the date and time.** Before fixing a day, check that there are no other events going on at the same time and avoid impractical periods such as the beginning of the school year, the day before bank holidays, the school holidays, etc. Let people know the date enough in advance in order to be sure of their availability. It is preferable to offer a workshop during the week, as the weekend is generally used as leisure time. In addition, consider organising your workshop in the low season, when rooms and hotels will be emptier and the prices will therefore be lower. As for the location, it is important to find a room that is suitable for all the logistics (video projector, internet access, comfort, possibility of bringing in a caterer, toilets, etc.). The quality of the room will vary depending on the workshop's importance. Nonetheless, a minimum level of comfort is required for the workshop to go well. Finally, the choice of location can always be made with consideration to its ease of access. Try to choose a site near a train station or airport.

> "For one of the workshops I have organised, we didn't have enough time to go to see the room in person. When we arrived on the day, we realised that the next-door room was having work done to it. It was so noisy that it was impossible to concentrate and work efficiently!" (Celine, project manager)

- **Set out a precise schedule** (this stage is even more important if the workshop is several days long). The objective here is to determine how long the workshop will last and how long the work sessions, practical activities, breaks, etc. will be. Be relatively flexible so that you can shorten or lengthen a session if necessary. The workshop's topic should be divided into several sections, in order to hold the participants' concentration: too much information and too many long sessions will make them lose their productivity and motivation. Leave nothing to chance and think about the times at which the participants will be the most attentive; it would be useless, for example, to explore the most difficult aspect of the subject before lunch or at the end of the day. A well-thought-out programme will give you a good overall view of the activities and will allow you to check that the workshop is running well each day. Do not hesitate to give the schedule to the speakers and experts for validation. An outside opinion is always welcome for identifying potential clashes or difficulties.

"During the last workshop I organised, while I was checking the plan for the day one final time, I realised that there was a problem in the schedule. One of the experts was not arriving until noon and his talk had been scheduled for 10am. Fortunately, it was 8am and we managed to quickly change the time and swap his talk with a work session from an expert who had arrived the day before!" (Selmi, production assistant)

The budget

Do not ignore the financial aspect of a workshop. Bringing together experts and participants for one or more days comes at a certain price. Calculate a pre-budget during your preparation so that you have the most precise estimation possible of future costs. If the workshop lasts several days, you can of course recalculate your budget during the event and readjust it if needed.

Then establish your priorities. Does the workshop need to be in a luxury hotel? Would cheaper accommodation not be sufficient? Think about this when it comes to catering too: do the experts and participants need fine dining? While the quality of meals should not be ignored, a five-star restaurant is perhaps unnecessary. Do not be surprised if some hotels refuse to lower the price of the bill. Try to gain some extra advantages in that case: additional comfort, a free luxury service, breakfast included, etc.

Technical organisation

The arrangement of your location is a determining factor in having a successful workshop. If you have a large group, such that you split off into smaller groups during some sessions, chose a room that can be divided into several spaces. Comfort should not be neglected, as it will allow the participants to concentrate more, and therefore be more inclined to exchange ideas.

It is also important to evaluate your technical needs and see if the room meets them. Is there a video projector? Are there enough plugs for everyone's laptop, if that is necessary to the workshop? Is the lighting suitable for a projection? When you visit these places, make a list of the material available there and of what you will need to provide yourselves. Finally, do not forget to take the experts wishes into account and, most importantly, test the internet connection as soon as you arrive.

During the workshop

If you have organised your workshop well, all you will have left to do on the day is set up the room and welcome the participants and experts. Nonetheless, as unforeseen circumstances might always arise, ensure that you arrive early enough to manage potential changes to the programme. Display the schedule prominently so that, when they arrive, the participants are up to date as to what is expected of them in the hours or days to come. The welcome is essential for getting off to a good start: smile, and warmly welcome everyone.

Once the workshop has begun, it is essential that the organiser does not miss their presentation. The role of the organiser or organisers is to accompany everyone so that no question goes unanswered. Their main role is to ensure that everything is clear to everyone. There are various ways of organising a workshop, depending on whether it is long or short. There are currently methods such as 'gamestorming', a technique for innovation and encouraging creativity through games. It was developed by Dave Gray, Sunni Brown and James Macanufo in their work *Gamestorming*, published in 2010. You might like the ASIT creative thinking method, which leads to innovative solutions, or the 'business war-game', mind mapping, 'creative problem solving', etc.

The following examples of activities can be used during your workshop:

- **The Phillips 6x6:** this exercise only works in large groups (at least 18 people). The organiser forms several groups of six and nominates a 'reporter'. The teams debate a topic for six minutes, then the reporters change groups, resume their previous discussion and thus relaunch the debate in their new circle. Once the first round is over, new reporters are designated and the game begins again. The aim of the exercise is to increase the topics of discussion and to be able to talk about them with all participants. For smaller workshops, a good variant of this game is the 'snowball', for which the participants are split into several groups of two. The first group debates an issue, then is joined by a second after ten minutes, and so on until all the duos have been grouped.
- **'Quescussion':** this simple exercise consists of leading a discussion solely in the form of questions. The aim is not to answer the question, but to clarify the attendees' ideas, allow them to better understand interviews and force them to better formulate their ideas. The individuals each take the floor in turn, so that everyone can express themselves.

During the workshop, do not forget downtime. Plan snacks and breaks throughout the day to break up the work and allow everyone to switch off for a few minutes. This will also encourage informal exchanges between attendees. If it is a long workshop (more than two days), plan moments of relaxation outside. Getting some fresh air and leaving the room or the hotel will be beneficial in the long run. You can also plan evening activities to strengthen relationships between participants.

Final evaluation

At the end of the workshop, do not forget to hand out an evaluation questionnaire to everyone present. This feedback will help you to determine what you need to improve. Focus your questionnaire on the understanding of objectives, the efficiency of the organisation, the atmosphere of the workshop and the organisation of the various talks. The best way to do this is with multiple choice questions. This evaluation, which should not be too long or complex, can also be done in the form of a debriefing, giving participants the floor and getting their impressions immediately. This exchange can in fact be rewarding for both participants and organisers. However, some people will be more comfortable and more honest with an anonymous questionnaire.

Satisfaction questionnaire

	Poor	Satisfactory	Good	Excellent
Quality of the reception				
Availability of information (schedule, etc.)				
Quality of the location (and ease of access)				
Quality of the equipment and premises				
Workshop atmosphere				
Understanding and approach of the theme				
Organisation of the workshop				
Quality of the speakers				
Quality of the food				
Knowledge and skills acquired				
What are, in your opinion, the main points to improve on?				

You do not need to wait until the end of the workshop to get to the evaluation. During the workshop, take note of anything that is causing a problem.

Once your workshop is over, it is important to get back to all the participants to confirm the success of the event: a word of thanks, a photo, a round-up report on the results, etc.

TOP TIPS

- **Check that all the equipment is working correctly** before the workshop. Get to the event location early (the day before if necessary), in order to check everything.
- **Contact the participants and experts a few days or weeks in advance,** in order to ensure that everyone will be there and to avoid unpleasant surprises on the first day.
- **Prepare for all situations.** Obviously, not everything will go as planned. Expect the unexpected and anticipate them so that you can react quickly and effectively in a crisis situation. For example, ask everyone if they have any dietary requirements or allergies. This will avoid trips to the emergency room in the middle of the workshop.
- **Feel free to rehearse,** that way you can be sure that you won't forget anything during the sessions and will seem confident to your participants. Additionally, you will feel more comfortable.
- **Have backup technical material** or a plan B in case a device breaks.
- **Arrange the room in a way that encourages interaction between participants,** in a circle or U-shape for example, so that everyone can see each other and exchange easily.
- **Maintain a good atmosphere among the group.** Use humour in your speeches, for example. Ensure there is a relaxed atmosphere to make the group feel comfortable.
- **Vary the methods used in the same working session.** Alternate difficult subjects with role play to keep the

participants focused. Additionally, pay attention to the times at which you schedule the most difficult topics. They will be better assimilated around 10am and 3pm.

> "We regularly use role play to make a workshop more exciting, fun and dynamic. It helps creativity!" (Celine, project manager)

- **Do not be stingy when it comes to media** (tables, graphics, etc.), as these will help the participants to focus on the topic at hand.
- **Show the order and schedule** so that they are visible to everyone. If adjustments are made during the workshop, make sure you draw attention to the new programme; a simple verbal announcement is not enough.
- **Offer activities outside of the workshop setting:** a restaurant meal, an outing at lunchtime, etc. This will encourage exchanges and strengthen the bonds between participants, who will then be more relaxed.

EMPLOYER ADVICE

To avoid awkwardness on the first day and to get off to a good start, give everyone a name badge. Everyone will know who they are talking to and contacts will be made more easily between the participants and the experts.

FAQS

WHAT ARE THE GOLDEN RULES FOR AN EFFECTIVE WORKSHOP?

When preparing a workshop, you must pay attention to a series of points, the 7Ps: establish the **Purpose** of the workshop and its target audience (**People**); consider the finished **Product** that you are looking for and the **Process** you will have to go through to get there; tackle the event's **Preparation** before concerning yourself with logistics or **Practical concerns**; and finally, the seventh P is the **Pitfalls** to avoid.

To be sure you haven't forgotten anything while preparing the workshop, follow these ten rules that are essential to the good organisation of this kind of event:

- Set the workshop's objectives and ask yourself what the event's purpose is;
- Define your target audience so that you can select your participants from it;
- Find a good title for your topic;
- Invite appropriate experts;
- Choose the appropriate location and room;
- Set a time and date and determine the duration of the workshop (one or more days);
- Send invitations to participants and experts sufficiently in advance;
- Prepare your provisional budget;
- Prepare a 'reverse schedule';

- Offer a welcome drink so that everyone can get to know each other better.

THINGS TO AVOID

Do not leave everything until the last minute, as a productive workshop requires preparation! The more you leave to the last minute, the more problems you will encounter and the less choice you will have when it comes to choosing a location, experts, technical material, etc. Some experts are so in demand that they are booked up months in advance. It is therefore preferable to start by sending invitations. Then, book the location so that you are not organising without any idea of where your workshop will be held.

HOW DO I CHOOSE THE PARTICIPANTS?

The participants will be chosen depending on what type of workshop it is and the objectives set by the organiser, but also depending on their motivation. For a workshop to be productive, those present must be sufficiently determined and want to make progress with other people. Select people based on their candidacy. The best thing to do is to ask for a letter of motivation so that you can see if the potential participant matches the profile of the workshop and whether they are sufficiently motivated. Then, carry out a personal interview so that you can be sure that the candidate will fit in during the workshop. To ensure there is a good group dynamic, the number of participants should be limited to around ten people, or several sub-groups of maximum ten people.

HOW CAN I ORGANISE A WORKSHOP THAT IS SEVERAL DAYS LONG?

During a long workshop (one or more days), it is a good idea to vary the angles from which you approach the topic so that nobody gets bored. This will also allow everyone to understand the subject better. The longer the workshop, the more time you should leave free in the schedule. Do not schedule days that are too long at the beginning and end of the workshop, so that participants and experts are not worn out and to ensure that the sessions go smoothly. Organise a meeting every morning with the organiser and the experts so that you do not forget anything.

HOW DO I KEEP THE PARTICIPANTS MOTIVATED THROUGHOUT THE EVENT?

The main rule for keeping groups motivated is being enthusiastic and dynamic yourself. Additionally, approach difficult subjects at times that are conducive to concentration (around 10am and 3pm). Do not forget to allow enough breaks to let the participants switch off for some time. Ensure that the environment is consistently positive so that motivation and good moods are catching.

HOW CAN I MANAGE UNFORESEEN CIRCUMSTANCES DURING THE WORKSHOP?

You can do this by planning as much as possible in advance. During the preparation stages, think about the risks and problems that could arise, and come up with solutions for them. The more prepared you are, the easier it will be to manage unexpected problems. Consider that, during the workshop, you will not have the time or space necessary to come up with a solution. Another way of decreasing risks is to have a 'dress rehearsal' before the workshop, if possible in the same location. You will then be able to see what is not working. Take time to test the material beforehand in order to avoid technical problems.

HOW IMPORTANT IS THE DEBRIEFING?

The debriefing allows you to gather everyone's impressions and encourages exchanges between the workshop's participants. A debriefing, however, is not enough to get to the heart of things. An evaluation questionnaire can be handed out to those present at the end of the workshop, in order to identify the positive and negative points in detail.

WHAT QUALITIES MUST A GOOD ORGANISER HAVE?

To organise a successful workshop, several skills are extremely useful: being diplomatic, being able to anticipate problems, being enthusiastic, knowing how to communicate well and resist stress, showing empathy, and being dynamic and versatile.

WHAT TECHNICAL ASPECTS MUST BE TAKEN INTO ACCOUNT?

The choice of location and room(s) that will host the workshop is essential. Check if the room has a video projector and a whiteboard. Make a list of the technical equipment you will need to provide. Ask yourself the right questions: does the room have reduced mobility access? Is it easily accessible by public transport? Is it adjustable to fit with the planned activities?

OVER TO YOU

YOUR CHECKLIST

So as not to forget anything when writing your checklist, consider each stage of the workshop, what you will need in every situation and the things to do to make sure everything is in order. Ask yourself the right questions and do not forget anything:

- **Preparation:** what is the theme of the workshop? What is its objective? Whom should you invite? When will you close sign-ups? Where will you organise the workshop? How long will it be?
- **Welcome:** what do you need to welcome the participants and speakers (logistics, documentation, technical equipment)? Will they need accommodation? Will they need to be collected from the train station or airport? When will you arrive at the location?
- **Organisation:** who is organising the workshop? At what time will the work sessions be? Which experts will you invite? What do you need (logistics, documentation, technical equipment)? What is the day's schedule? Should you organise an outing or a restaurant meal for the evening?
- **Communication:** when will you send the invitations? Do you need to advertise? Should you launch a website for the event? Who will be in charge of this?

Checklist example

Workshop preparation

- ☐ Set objectives
- ☐ Find a catchy title
- ☐ Identify target audience
- ☐ Choose experts
- ☐ Send invitations
- ☐ Choose date
- ☐ Book room
- ☐ Create schedule
- ☐ Advertise on business's website

Logistical aspects

- ☐ Calculate provisional budget
- ☐ Check available material
- ☐ Ask speakers about their requirements
- ☐ Make a list of material needed
- ☐ Check internet connection
- ☐ Book caterer
- ☐ Write evaluation questionnaire
- ☐ Book restaurant for outing

On the day

- ☐ Check material
- ☐ Prepare welcome drinks
- ☐ Put up the schedule where everyone can see it
- ☐ Collect experts from the airport

At the same time as you are making your checklist, write down the cost of each stage, task, reservation, so that you have an idea of your provisional budget. Remember to deduct the amount charged to the participants for signing up.

REVERSE SCHEDULE

To make your reverse schedule, consider each task that needs to be done and, starting with the project's end date, work backwards to figure out when each task must be finished by, at the latest. Do this in the form of a table – preferably Excel – so that you can easily see the deadlines for each of them.

Reverse schedule example

Task to complete	Person	Deadline
Choose subject		
Choose date		
Choose location		
Book location		
Establish provisional budget		
Launch website (or publish information on existing website)		
Open sign-ups		
Close sign-ups		
Select participants		
Invite experts		
Book transport		
Book hotels		
Create schedule		
Print programme		
Organise outings/restaurants		
Prepare material		
Prepare bills		
Send evaluation questionnaires		
Assess and settle accounts		
Examine evaluation sheets		
Write a report		
Etc.		

DRESS REHEARSAL

A few days before the event, go to the workshop's location (if you can) and plan each action. Where are you going to put the welcome table? Where will your desk be? Prepare your welcome speech and practise it out loud, if possible in front of your assistant or colleague. Check the room's layout and see where you can display the schedule. These actions will help you to see what you have forgotten and what there is left to do before the big day.

We want to hear from you!
Leave a comment on your online library
and share your favourite books on social media!

FURTHER READING

BIBLIOGRAPHY

- Manager-Go. (2013) *Conduire un workshop.* [Online]. [Accessed 1 July 2015]. Available from: <http://www.manager-go.com/gestion-de-projet/dossiers-methodes/conduire-un-workshop>
- Finot, J.-F. (2009) Organiser un workshop, les règles d'or. *Neoxia.* [Online]. [Accessed 1 July 2015]. Available from: <http://blog.neoxia.com/organiser-un-workshop-les-regles-dor/>
- Gedalge, P. (2014) Qu'est-ce qui rend un groupe efficace. *Hbrfrance.* [Online]. [Accessed 1 July 2015]. Available from: <http://www.hbrfrance.fr/chroniques-experts/2014/12/5314-questce-qui-rend-un-groupe-efficace/>
- Asso-Alpe. (No date) *Les techniques d'animation.* [Accessed 1 July 2015]. Available from: <http://www.asso-alpe.fr/fichiers/martial/pagejoueraquoi/technique-sanimation.pdf>
- Macanufo, J., Brown, S. and Gray, D. (2010) *Gamestorming: a Playbook for Innovators, Rulebreakers, and Changemakers.* New York: O'Reilly.
- Asit. *Méthode de créativité ASIT.* [Online]. [Accessed 21 July 2015]. Available from: <http://www.asit.info/>
- Metiu, A. and Rothbard, N. P. (2012) Task Bubbles, Artifacts, Shared Emotion, and Mutual Focus of Attention: A Comparative Study of The Microprocesses of Group Engagement. *Organization Science.* [Online]. [Accessed 1 July 2015]. Available from: <http://pubson-

line.informs.org/doi/10.1287/orsc.1120.0738>

- Pacaud, T. (no date) Conseils pour organiser un séminaire ou un workshop idéal. *Team4Development.* [Online]. [Accessed 1 July 2015]. Available from: <http://www.team4development.fr/conseils-pour-organiserun-seminaire-ou-un-workshop-ideal/>
- Santrot, F. (2005) Dix règles d'or pour organiser un événement professionnel. *Journal du Net.* [Online]. [Accessed 1 July 2015]. Available from: <http://www.journaldunet.com/management/0511/0511109evenementiel.shtml>

ADDITIONAL SOURCES

- Candelo R., C. (2003) *Organising and running workshops.* [Online]. [Accessed 10 November 2016]. Available from:< http://www.gwp.org/global/gwp-sam_files/publicaciones/organising-and-running-workshops-a-practical-guide-for-trainers.pdf>
- Dearling, A. (2003) *Organising Successful Learning Events.* Lyme Regis: Russell House Publishing.
- *MindTools*: Planning a Workshop - https://www.mindtools.com/pages/article/PlanningAWorkshop.htm

IMPROVE YOUR GENERAL KNOWLEDGE

IN A BLINK OF AN EYE !

www.50minutes.com

www.50minutes.com

Ebook EAN: 9782806288844

Paperback EAN: 9782806288851

Legal Deposit: D/2016/12603/725

Cover: © Primento

Digital conception by Primento, the digital partner of publishers.